Uncommon Trust

Learning to Trust God when Life Doesn't Make Sense

Erik Reed

kjmin.org

Cover design: The A Group

Cover image: The A Group

First printing: 2021

Printed in the United States of America

Unless otherwise indicated, Scripture quotations are from the ESV Bible (The Holy Bible, English Standard Version), copyright 2001 by Crossway, a publishing ministry of Good News Publishers. Used by permission. All rights reserved.

All emphases in Scripture quotations have been added by the author.

ISBN: 9798506998280

To Katrina, who has displayed a picture of trusting in the LORD through the worst circumstances any mother could endure. You are stronger in your faith than most will ever know. I'm thankful God put us together to walk this journey.

CONTENTS

ENDORSEMENTS

"Erik Reed has written a heartfelt, accessible book on suffering and the sovereignty of God. Soaked in the Scriptures and borne from personal experience, Erik's challenge will lead you closer to the God who loves and holds us."

- Trevin Wax
Author of *Rethink Your Self*, *This Is Your Time*, and *Gospel Centered Teaching*

"Suffering is often what I see drive people away from their faith. My friend, Pastor Erik Reed, had the opposite experience. While experiencing great pain and sorrow in the trials and then death of his son Kaleb, Erik has the credibility to claim we should "trust in the Lord" in our suffering, and what that actually means for the Christian life, beyond the coffee mug clichè. Erik is someone I would call a "hopeful sufferer," which is the very thing God has prescribed for us in our pain. With gospel-centered insight from the scriptures and real life experience, Erik is the right person to take on this very personal and important topic. I will be giving this book to church members, and thank God it has been written."

- Dean Inserra
Pastor at City Church, Tallahassee, author of *The UnSaved Christian* and *Getting Over Yourself*

"In an age of surface-level 'Deconstruction' narratives and 'ex-vangelical' diatribes, Pastor Erik Reed has done something critical for the church by providing an accessible volume dealing with the difficult topics of suffering, sovereignty, and the glory of Christ. What Erik does is demonstrate something profound—how it's our acquaintance with grief that truly plumbs the depth of God's goodness in ways that milquetoast Christianity never could. In cutting through the truisms, we see the veneer of easy-believism strip away, and what's left is the raw exposure of a trusting faith."

- **Andrew T. Walker**
Associate Professor of Christian Ethics at The Southern Baptist Theological Seminary, Author of *God and the Transgender Debate*

"Erik Reed has modeled, up close, what it looks like to endure the worst possible suffering. Our faith is tested most when we endure the worst and for Erik, he has emerged not only with his faith intact, but with a powerful and biblical apologetic for trusting in the goodness of God. If you have endured deep suffering, if you know someone who has endured deep suffering, please read this book. Too much of our modern versions of Christianity live off a diet of cheap promises of endless happiness, but this book points us back to the richness of life in the valley, life in Christ. You will want to read this book and give it to others."

- **Dan Darling**
Senior VP at NRB, author of several books including, *A Way With Words*, *The Dignity Revolution* and *The Characters of Christmas*.

"Recounting his own journey through the valley of shadow, Erik Reed issues a call to all believers to trust in God in every seemingly insurmountable situation we face in life. Dealing with some of life's most probing and spiritual questions, *Uncommon Trust* offers us a deep well from which to draw to receive the cool refreshing waters of biblical truth amid the parched lands of suffering. From drawing back the veil on the glorious attributes of God to exploring why we mistakenly choose to lean upon our own understanding and resources, this work is sure to help you discover the peaceful pastures of our faithful Good Shepherd. The message of this timely work is simple, trust him, even when your world may be falling apart, trust him."

- Dustin Benge
Provost and professor of historical and pastoral theology at Union School of Theology, Bridgend and Oxford, UK.

"Most people are familiar with Christian platitudes that get thrown around in the midst of pain. Just "trust in the Lord" they tell you, while you're wondering how you'll make it through another day of grief and sorrow. This book takes that well-intentioned idea and builds a foundation underneath it that you can actually stand on. It's true, you can "trust in the Lord," and Erik Reed shows you how."

- Costi W. Hinn
Author of *More Than a Healer*, President/Founder of For the Gospel

The common habit of the Christian is the habit of trusting.

— Charles Spurgeon

1

THE GREAT EXPOSER

Do you trust the LORD? Do you trust Him with your life and circumstances? Do you trust Him with your future? Do you trust Him when pain, sorrow, and suffering come your way? If so, you know the peace, comfort, and contentment trusting the LORD brings in your life. If you don't trust Him, or you find yourself hesitant to affirm full trust in any area of your life, then you recognize the stress, worry, and fear, that lack of trust breeds. Failing to trust the LORD breeds unrest and turmoil as we navigate the troubles and trials of life.

The natural question is: How does trust in the LORD develop? How do we get to the place where our hearts trust God amid life's problems?

Most people will eventually encounter fear, anxiety, and worry. Some will struggle with depression, difficulty forgiving people, and doubts about whether their marriage will survive. Many will struggle to understand why they've experienced divorce, addiction, cancer, financial hardship, career setbacks, infertility, the inability to find Mr. or Mrs. Right, and other things. These troubles pervade life in a broken and fallen world.

As you read this, you may immediately identify with one or more of these issues. And if you do relate to them, know that these things are not uncommon at all. They are a normal part of the human experience for all people, Christians included. What is uncommon is for those who are hurting to experience peace in their hearts despite their troubles. What is uncommon today are people dealing with afflictions with hearts at rest.

PASTORAL ENCOUNTERS

Pastoring has brought me into many difficult situations people face. I've sat with parents after a child's surgery to hear the news that the cancer was more advanced than they thought. I've comforted people who discovered their spouse was having an affair. Many times, I've joined families as a loved one passed into eternity, and into God's presence. The list goes on and on. The point of mentioning it is that such circumstances often demonstrate whether those individuals and families trust the LORD. Every Christian knows trusting God is basic to the faith, but it's in trials where the substance of our trust manifests.

In other words, trials and tribulations expose our actual level of trust in God. They wipe away mere words about trusting the LORD and get to the reality. Suffering is the great exposer.

Several years ago, I spoke with a church member who struggled to understand something that happened to her as a young girl. When she was in junior high, a teacher molested her. Time moved on, and she eventually believed it no longer affected her. But when her own children reached the same age, feelings of anger surfaced, as well as questions about God's sovereignty.

She wrestled with questions like: "Why would God allow such a thing? How could that be God's will?" Someone once tried to comfort her by saying, "Oh, honey, that's not God's doing. That's an evil man in a broken world."

She agreed with their second sentence, but she followed up with, "God had the power to stop or prevent it, but He didn't. If God allows a wicked deed, He's still willing it to happen, even if just passively."

When I met with her, her question centered on why, if God had the power to stop it, He chose not to. What purpose does God have in suffering? How do we grasp His will in things we know He hates?

As we talked, the issue centered on what it always does: trust. When we don't understand what God is doing or why God acts as He does, will we choose to trust Him instead of understanding Him? If God doesn't show us how He is working through our troubles, will we harden our hearts toward Him? Will we choose to trust Him or accuse Him?

You may think this sounds callous or insensitive, but it's the furthest thing from that. I'm speaking as someone who has grappled with all the same questions. My family has had a front seat on the road of suffering.

LEARNING FIRSTHAND

My wife, Katrina, and I got word that our girls had arrived at the hospital. We sent everyone out of Kaleb's room. I walked to the lobby to meet them, dreading the news I had to share. Kaleigh was ten, and Kyra was six. Their fifteen-year-old brother, Kaleb, was their hero. We walked hand-in-hand down the hallway until we reached his room. They perceived something abnormal was happening. I pulled them aside before entering and got down on my knees in front of them.

"Girls," my voice cracked as I choked up, "your brother is very sick. And he's not getting better. He's going to go be with Jesus today." They burst into tears and hugged me. We sat there crying for a few minutes. Katrina was in the room with Kaleb loving on him, rubbing his head. I told the girls, "We're going into Bubba's room to love on him and tell him how much we love him."

Over the next hour we said goodbye and made final

memories together as a family of five. The rest of our family and friends joined us in the room as we read Scripture, sang songs of hope, and watched as the weight of glory engulfed Kaleb's present sufferings. His faith became sight.

Kaleb's death on December 1, 2019 was the end of his lifetime of trials and afflictions. He was born only 30 weeks into the pregnancy. The cause of his complications was a bad kidney filled with cysts. Doctors wanted to let him grow and get stronger before removing the bad kidney, but the kidney caused problems each day it remained in his body. After two months in the hospital and several infections later, the doctors moved ahead with a surgery to remove the bad kidney. They assured us the bad dream ended after the procedure and that a normal life with one kidney awaited. The prospect of a normal life sounded wonderful.

Things appeared fine after the surgery. We waited for him to pee so we could get his discharge papers from the hospital. The first day passed—no pee. The second day passed—no pee. His blood pressure rose, and his heart rate increased by the hour. Doctors and nurses began to look concerned, but said nothing. They ordered an ultrasound and MRI to probe further.

Within a few hours, the surgeon that removed Kaleb's kidney came to our room and informed us, "We not only took his bad kidney, but we took the good kidney by mistake. It's unfortunate."

The shock you just felt as you read that? That was our response too, but multiplied exponentially.

Mistake? Unfortunate?

The news devastated us. Those words, and the reality they brought with them, turned our lives upside down. A team of doctors huddled with us that night to provide options about Kaleb's care. The first option was to insert a catheter and try dialysis until he was big enough to receive a kidney transplant. His hospital, a leading children's hospital in the nation, had never done this on a child his size or age. The second option was to do nothing—let him die.

We chose the first option.

Kaleb did dialysis while waiting to get a kidney transplant. We spent so much time in the hospital. He almost died multiple times. Infections, blood clots, and broken catheters were regular occurrences. But we kept going, and two years after his botched surgery, he received his mom's kidney.

The kidney transplant changed our lives. He required many medications and dealt with multiple health complications, but compared to his first two years, it was an improvement.

Kaleb lived like every typical boy. He attended school, played tee-ball and hockey, and loved gaming with his friends. He played on the school basketball team in junior high and got in trouble when he lost his homework. His favorite sports teams were the

Nashville Predators, Golden State Warriors, and Tennessee Vols football. We enjoyed life as a family. From the time Kaleb was two until age thirteen, nobody comprehended the severity of his medical issues unless they knew him or his story.

Kaleb had an infectious laugh and smile despite all his pains. People often questioned how it was possible. There's one answer: Jesus. He had a personal relationship and deep abiding trust in Jesus. We spoke often about life's hardships, and how Jesus reigned over everything. He understood God used his story to teach others. I shared his testimony to tens of thousands of students over the years and often brought him on stage with me.

But in October 2017, everything changed again. Kaleb experienced trouble with his vision and some other neurological issues. We took him to the hospital for tests, but within a few days he was unconscious. They discovered he had fungal meningitis and had suffered two strokes. He remained unconscious for the next three weeks. We had no assurances he would survive, or about his condition if he did.

They treated Kaleb with aggressive medications to kill the meningitis, and after three weeks, he regained consciousness. But the strokes caused severe damage, affecting his speech and motor skills. All told, we stayed in the hospital and rehab facility for over 90 days. By the end, Kaleb had recovered significant motor skills. He walked with help and used his limbs moderately well. But his speech didn't improve. We hoped his progress would continue in the months ahead, that he would regain most of his previous abilities. But in the months following his discharge from the hospital and rehab facility, grueling pain developed in his legs. Doctors struggled to discover the source, but they had no success. Kaleb's physical progress deteriorated, leaving him completely dependent on us to care for him.

These were hard days. His excruciating pain found no relief unless we gave him medicines that made him sleep all day. It was awful. On top of the neurological pain, his lungs stayed lodged with secretions because he could no longer cough on command. His lungs acted like those of a cystic fibrosis patient, even though he didn't have the disease. Doctors prescribed more medications and treatments to help keep his lungs clear, but it grew more and more difficult.

In November 2019, Kaleb's low oxygen levels put him in the hospital once again. This wasn't new for him. He developed lung infections multiple times per year throughout his life. The pattern: get admitted to the hospital, receive treatments, recover, and go home. But this time Kaleb didn't get better. His lungs had nothing left.

Years of fighting and overcoming obstacles left his body fatigued. On the morning of December 1, after speaking with multiple doctors about our options, Katrina and I chose not to put our son through any more surgeries or treatments due to the condition of his lungs. The conversation devastated us, but we had peace it was the right decision. We didn't want Kaleb to suffer any longer. We wanted him free from his struggles—and with Jesus.

We suffered with him throughout his life, but his death wasn't the end of our afflictions. It only created a new one: learning to live without a child you love so much.

ANXIETY STRIKES

Why do I share this story? Because it's important for you, the reader, to know that I'm not only sharing lessons from the Bible about trusting God, but I've lived it on a personal level. I've walked—and I'm still walking—in the throes of pain and sorrow. I understand the anxieties, fears, heaviness, and unsettling nature of suffering and affliction. Trials and struggles have been a regular traveler with me and my family.

But throughout many years of pastoring people through pain, facing Kaleb's death, and studying God's Word, I've developed a theology of suffering. I've learned how to walk through the fires without losing faith or confidence in God. I know what it means to trust in the LORD when you don't understand His will, even when His plans hurt.

However, I wasn't always there. In 2004, several months after Kaleb's surgical mistake, I had my first panic attack. The event was unfamiliar; I thought I was dying. "Am I going crazy?", I thought to myself. I loved Jesus, and was growing as a Christian, but I lacked the tools to handle the stress and newfound anxiety in my life. The onset of panic attacks started years of seeking peace and comfort despite our family's trials. I sought the Lord, searched the Scriptures, and developed a plan for finding help.

And I did.

It didn't magically fix my circumstances. But it did change my perspective and heart. And since then, I've helped many people facing similar struggles.

Maybe that's where you are today. Your faith is wavering and wobbling because of trials, troubles, or pains. Perhaps somebody suggested this book to you because of the circumstances you're facing now or went through in the past. I believe God has placed this book in your hands. In His divine providence, this book has landed in your possession and you've read this far (congratulations!) because He intends to help you through your struggles. God wants to equip His people to trust Him through whatever He brings their way.

I'm burdened by the number of Christians unprepared to handle life's sorrows and pain. Many sincere followers of Jesus have delusions that their lives will remain free of major troubles. When those false ideas crumble under the weight of invading problems, it leaves many Christians disoriented and questioning where God was when the storm rolled through. They become disillusioned when what they perceived life would be like gives way to what it actually is.

WHAT'S THE ANSWER?

What is the answer to finding peace and comfort during life's struggles? What is the remedy for the countless troubles that plague our lives? Here it is: Trust in the LORD.

That's the answer. It sounds too simplistic to be practical, right? But it's true. Trusting in the LORD brings peace and comfort amid ten thousand things that trouble our souls.

So how do we do it? This book aims to answer that question and help you trust in the LORD. My prayer is that it helps you avoid grumbling under the weight of suffering and sorrows, or if you're there now, that it serves as a life raft to save you from drowning in your anger, bitterness, and resentment toward God. I want you to experience the hope, peace, and joy that comes from trusting God—with all your heart—even when life makes no sense.

Discussion Questions

1. Why is learning to trust God in this world so difficult, even for Christians?

2. What have been some hinderances in your life from trusting God? What things that have happened in your past still play a role in keeping you from trusting in the LORD?

3. As you heard Kaleb's story, and considered the trials he endured in his life, do you think you trusting God has more to do with the severity of your trials and pain or is it tied more to your knowledge and fellowship with Him?

4. This chapter talked the about anxiety and panic attacks I experienced as a result of the trials endured with Kaleb's health. What kind of emotional struggles do you find present in your own life (anxiety, fear, worry, depression, low self-esteem, etc.)?

5. Learning to trust in the LORD is the key for finding peace in the midst of life's pains. Do you believe the majority of Christians have learned to trust God through whatever they endure in life?

6. What are you hoping God will teach and show you as you read this book?

2

TRUSTING GOD

"Just trust God." That's a common response people hear from other believers when they're facing troubles. These believers mean well. Their motives are pure. But is this actually helpful advice for those suffering afflictions?

Yes, and no. The counsel to "trust the LORD" is correct, and a much-needed reality in our lives. We would have more peace and contentment if our trust in the LORD increased. If we refused to let our trials and troubles deter us from trusting God, our emotional highs and lows would dissipate.

The Bible tells us to trust the LORD. So, when we counsel others to trust God we are giving them truth.

Trust in the LORD with all your heart, and do not lean on your own understanding. In all your ways acknowledge him, and he will make straight your paths.
— *Proverbs 3:5-6*

Many people are familiar with Proverbs 3:5-6. It's popular. It's often on coffee mugs, bumper stickers, and t-shirts. But well known doesn't mean well understood. It's possible to be very familiar with a passage without comprehending it. Proverbs 3:5-6 is a cliché for some people. We encourage people with it who are suffering, and receive it as counsel from others, without knowing the meaning. For that reason, the advice rarely achieves its desired outcome, not because it lacks capacity to help, but because people don't know how it helps.

TRUST IN THE LORD

Notice the first words of this passage are an exhortation: "Trust in the LORD." It's a command. We are told to do something; it requires our action. The verb "trust" means to rely on. To trust is to rely on the character, strength, or truth of the object in question. It's placing confidence in something.

When we travel on an airplane, we board the massive aluminum tube, trusting in its character, strength, and reliability to get us to our destination. If we didn't trust the plane to do that, we wouldn't buy tickets. (That's why some people don't.) Or another example, every time we sit on a chair, we rely on that chair to hold our weight. We're depending on the character, strength, and reliability of the chair to fulfill its job—keeping us off the floor. Sitting on an airplane or a chair is placing our confidence in those objects.

The same is true for trusting God. It's banking on the character, strength, and reliability of who He is. It's placing our confidence in Him—infinitely more reliable than a chair or plane.

The original Hebrew word for trust in this passage paints the picture of lying helplessly, face downward. Trust is giving oneself up to the mercy of another. It's vulnerability. It's putting down your guard. That's the picture of trust. The writer of the proverb describes our trust as being "with all our heart." This is the nature of it. It's not with a begrudging heart. We don't give the LORD half-hearted trust. We trust with our whole being, full throttle, with everything. We hold nothing back, leaving nothing in reserve.

Before I go further, consider your own life. As you observe the landscape of your heart, and examine your life, do you detect that kind of trust in the LORD? When the Lord looks upon your heart, does He discover the heart of one who fully, and without hesitation, trusts in Him? Our Creator deserves our total trust, in every aspect of our lives, with every fiber of our being.

DO NOT LEAN

The writer contrasts trusting the LORD with the next statement: "and do not lean on your own understanding." This is the picture of resting on something for our support. If you lean your body against a wall, you're expecting the wall to support you.

To lean on our own understanding is to let our own comprehension of circumstances sit in the driver's seat of our thoughts. It's letting our minds fabricate stories to interpret our situation. It's us trying to predict our futures. And it's dangerous.

When we're facing trials and troubles, fears about the future surface. Instead of trusting in the LORD, we lean on what we can grasp or understand. Imagine a rickety bridge like you see in movies, hundreds of feet over a ravine, with wood-plank steps and ropes for handrails. Below the bridge is a river with large, jagged-edge rocks protruding through the rushing waters. Now picture yourself walking across that bridge. Would you feel confident to lean on the loose ropes and thrust all your weight backward against them? No, right? Few people would view those ropes as secure.

That is the danger of leaning on your own understanding. Relying on your own ability to make sense of your circumstances is risky. Angst about tomorrow plagues our hearts when troubles swirl around us. We fear the future. The unspoken question that troubles us is what the end of this passage talks about: "He will make straight our paths." He will guide our lives according to His plan. Even when we struggle with our past hurts, it's usually because we fear they could repeat. We tell ourselves, "If it happened once, it could happen again." We reason, "If this happened to that person, it could happen to us." Our hope is for a straight path. And we want it to be

17

straight according to our definition.

Our struggles stem from our lack of control. We don't control tomorrow. We don't control next week, next month, or next year. That sobering truth leads us to deal with the realities of our weaknesses, helplessness, and impotence. These things confront us with a decision point: Will we trust in the LORD or lean on our own understanding? Later in the book, I'll devote an entire chapter to how this process unfolds and how we can fight to trust in the LORD rather than ourselves.

A HUMAN PROBLEM

This is where most people live. I wish only non-Christians struggled with this, and that Christians had it all figured out. But we don't. Most Christians live in this struggle too. It's as common as homeschool kids working at Chick-fil-A. Most people live leaning on their own understanding as their default mode. Many Christians lack peace in the midst of pain because they lean on their own understanding. In fact, most people grapple with crippling depression, fear, and anxiety because they are leaning on their own understanding.

It's a massive problem.

As some of you read this, your inner lawyer rises to your defense, "I don't do that!" But when you examine how you emotionally handle things you can't control, and uncertainties that accompany life, are you at peace or do you worry?

My aim isn't to condemn you or wag the finger of judgment in your face. I want to help. I want the people of God to live in freedom, not fear. Christians can live at peace (instead of panic) through life's troubles. We can remain steady when confronted with the reality that we don't control the future. Rather than fear ruling us, we can live confident in God's plan for our future, even if we've experienced past hurts and troubles.

After facing recurring anxiety attacks, the question surfaced for me: Am I going to live like this my entire life? I was in my mid-twenties and the thought of living sixty more years with constant panic attacks and anxiety terrified me. I couldn't comprehend such a life. That's when I realized I had to do business with God.

I had to learn how to trust in the LORD. And I did. It was a seven-year (messy and frustrating!) process, but I reached a point where my number of panic attacks declined, and then disappeared. And by the grace of God, it's been years since my last panic attack. How did that happen? What brought the change? Learning to trust God.

A DISCOVERY

This book teaches how you can grow to trust in the LORD. The emphasis there is on "grow." Trusting God isn't something we turn off and on like a light switch. We can't generate it by sheer force of will. It's developed, grown, and nurtured day by day. It happens through a relationship with God.

The Christian life isn't about simply believing in God, but knowing Him. It's not only about placing faith in Jesus for salvation, but walking in a relationship with Him that changes everything. Christ died and rose from the dead to save sinners and reconcile us to God (1 Peter 3:18), and the reconciliation doesn't begin in eternity, but here and now. It leads us to a daily relationship with God. Communion and fellowship with God is how trust in Him is nurtured.

Why is this so crucial to grasp? Because if we neglect close fellowship with God—where trust is cultivated—we can't conjure it up when a crisis emerges. It's either there or not. This idea emerges from Proverbs 3:5-6. We are to trust "in" the LORD. It's the character and person of God that garners our trust. The passage says, "in all our ways acknowledge him." To acknowledge the Lord isn't to tip our cap at Him. It isn't mentioning Him at the end of an acceptance speech. To acknowledge is to "know." It signifies fellowship with Him. In all our ways, have fellowship with God, know Him, and He will make your path straight.

Think about it. It makes sense when we stop to reflect. How do we develop trust with people in our lives? We're in relationship with them. The more we know someone, the more we learn whether we can or can't trust them. Why is this? Because the greater we know someone, the clearer their character becomes to us. Trust is about relying on the character of someone or something.

FELLOWSHIP WITH HIM

The same is true with trusting God. Our path for growing in trust is engaging in an ongoing relationship with God. The byproduct and fruit of pursuing a relationship with God is that our trust blossoms and flourishes. As this happens, more peace and contentment accompanies us through life's trials.

Growing in relationship and knowledge of God happens the same way it does with anyone else: We spend time with Him. Christians must prioritize daily time with God. He is always near us, and we're never separated from Him. But it's important to set aside uninterrupted time to commune with Him.

What do we do with that time?

Pray. Speak with the Lord. Honor Him as God, and give thanks for His blessings and kindness to you. Ask Him to grow your faith and take your needs to Him. Pray for others. The key to healthy prayer is not how beautiful or eloquent our words are, but bringing our hearts to Him.

Read Scripture. Consider following a Bible reading plan. The issue isn't how much we read, but the quality of our reading. We should read Scripture to have God reveal Himself, His will, and His ways to us. Our prayer as we read should echo David's prayer from Psalm 119:18, "Open my eyes, that I may behold wondrous things out of your law." God reveals who He is, in His nature and character, through Scripture. This is vital for growing in trust, because we don't want to trust in the God of our own making—a god based on our opinions or pop-culture depictions. God reveals Himself through the Scriptures, and we fellowship with Him as we read them.

Embrace Community. We also experience fellowship with God through corporate worship in our churches and by living in community with other believers. As we worship and grow together, the Lord reveals Himself among us.

These are several examples of ways we spend time with the Lord. When we spend time with Him, we grow to trust Him more and more.

INTO DAD'S ARMS

As a father of three children, I've done my fair share of making my kids jump off of high places so I can catch them. I'm not sure why dads, more than moms, love doing this. But we do. It's our thing.

When I've done this with Kaleb, Kaleigh, and Kyra, they've all been hesitant to jump on my first countdown to leap into my arms. I go through the routine, "1... 2... 3... jump!" Nothing. They hesitate. "C'mon," I say, "I've got you!" Then the routine starts over again. After several minutes of reluctance from the kids, and several minutes of me reminding them I will catch them, they finally jump. I've experienced this same thing with each of my kids.

Now imagine after minutes of hesitating to trust me by not jumping, they leap from whatever surface I placed them on, and I moved out of the way and let them hit the ground. Imagine me staring at them on the ground and telling them, "You should have jumped the first time. This is what you get."

This would disqualify any man from a "Father of the Year" award. No good father would do that. No matter how much hem-hawing or fear a child displays before jumping, a good father catches his kids when they finally do.

God catches His children too.

If you recognize that you've not been trusting God with your life, you can turn to Him even now. He won't reject you because of your previous failures to trust. He doesn't let us fall to the ground because of our struggles to trust Him in the past. He catches us. Failure to trust Him with our lives in the past shouldn't keep us from trusting Him today. Turn to Him. Make the leap. He promises to catch you. You can trust Him.

The irony is after a child finally jumps, and trusts their father to catch them, they're hooked. That father spends the next five minutes catching his kid, looking for a way to stop what he started. The act of trusting him, and discovering that he's trustworthy, breeds more trust. This is also how it works in our walk with God. The more we step out and trust Him in our circumstances, the more we discover that He's trustworthy. And each time encourages us to trust Him more.

THE JOURNEY AHEAD

In the pages ahead, we're studying the Scriptures to see, and behold, the God who meets us there. We want to explore His attributes and nature. That's how we build trust. We are looking at specific aspects of His character that help foster and develop our trust in Him. These attributes include God's wisdom, love, and faithfulness. But the first character trait we'll study, and the one I believe is most vital to grasp in our quest to trust Him through all of life's troubles, is the sovereignty of God. It's to that subject we now turn.

Discussion Questions

1. What is something you worry about or try to control? What is the thing, that when it comes up, causes you to stop trusting God and revert to leaning on your own understanding?

2. "Trust in the LORD" is a command. If we really trust the LORD with our salvation, why do we struggle to trust Him with our daily issues? What does it look like to truly trust the LORD?

3. Discuss some ways to develop trust in the LORD (Psalm 37:4-6, Romans 8:28, Psalm 28:7, Matthew 6:25).

4. When you look upon the landscape of your heart, and examine your life, do you find that kind of trust in the LORD? What does God see? Discuss some ways to stop being self-reliant.

5. How have things turned out when you truly leaned on your own understanding. Discuss the benefits of not leaning on your own understanding and trusting the LORD (Psalm 125:1, Psalm 62:8, Jeremiah 17:5-9).

6. Discuss what you think it means for God to make our paths straight. What might that look like?

3

THE SOVEREIGNTY OF GOD

Have you ever heard a story about someone that didn't match what you knew about them? For example, I despise Taco Bell. They use the lowest quality meat allowed by federal regulations (not confirmed, but probably true). So if someone tells you they saw me at Taco Bell, elbow deep in tacos, with a giant smile on my face and hot sauce on my clothes, you have good reason to doubt the story's accuracy. Why? Because you know I hate Taco Bell.

This relates to our trust in God. There are specific attributes of God's character that—when we know them—breed trust. Knowing His character helps us when we go through trials and pains. We intensify most of our worries and fears by a lack of knowing God. Inch deep belief in God doesn't deter the crippling effects suffering and sorrows produce.

The Bible does not tell us to trust God because our circumstances will always unfold according to our hopes. It's because things happen the way God plans, and most times, we won't understand His reasons. We must place deep and abiding confidence in the God "who is over all and through all and in all" (Ephesians 4:6).

SOVEREIGN

God's sovereignty is the first attribute we must know to grow in trust in Him. The sovereignty of God is His authority and control over His creation. Abraham Kuyper said, "There is not a square inch in the whole domain of our human existence over which Christ, who is Sovereign over all, does not cry, Mine!" People call kings and queens sovereign. They rule and reign over a land and people. But God's sovereignty stretches over all things.

His sovereignty includes the power to do all that He pleases. Nothing can thwart or disrupt God's plans. God never wonders what He's going to do. Nothing happens outside of His will or beyond His control. In other words, nothing happens without His willing it to happen, and willing it to happen in the way it happens.

The sovereignty of God is a like a sparkling diamond that refracts colors and brilliance as light shines off its many facets. God is sovereign over every aspect of life, and like a diamond, as we turn it around and let the light hit different facets, its brilliance is displayed. The sovereignty of God, when understood, produces awe and wonder. It's beautiful! In this chapter, I want to present several facets of the sovereignty of God, and let them sink into our hearts.

OVER NATURAL ELEMENTS

God rules over His creation. Wind, clouds, and oceans are in His hands. Scripture testifies throughout that the Lord is sovereign over what He has made. Genesis 1 shows creation responding to the will of God. By his command, He spoke, and creation came into existence. When God spoke, His will materialized. God's desire to create a universe, and His speaking that universe into being, happened without debate.

As God saw sin and rebellion from humanity in the world, He showed His sovereignty over creation again.

For behold, I will bring a flood of waters upon the earth to destroy all flesh in which is the breath of life under heaven. — Genesis 6:17

God didn't predict a flood, nor did He get a glimpse of the pending weather forecast and decide to use it as an instrument of judgment on the earth. The text says, "I will bring a flood." The LORD directs the event. What proceeded was 40 days and 40 nights of rain.

In Exodus 14:26-27, Moses leads the people of Israel out of Egypt. The LORD tells Moses to strike the water, causing the Red Sea to part so the Israelites can pass through on dry ground. Once they reached safety, God sent the walls of water crashing down onto the Egyptian soldiers pursuing God's people. This is all the Lord's doing.

When the prophet Jonah runs from God's call to preach to Nineveh, the LORD responded to his attempt to flee to Tarshish instead of obey.

But the LORD hurled a great wind upon the sea, and there was a mighty tempest on the sea, so that the ship threatened to break up. — Jonah 1:4

Jonah runs from God's command, but God hurls a great wind upon the sea, causing the waves to reach epic sizes. Anybody cruising the ocean that day would conclude a natural storm was brewing. But Scripture brings us behind the curtain to see God's actions. And regarding the ocean, Job 38:11 tells us God determines the boundaries of the water and dry land when He declared, "This far and no farther."

Jesus displays power over creation in Matthew 8. He is sleeping when a massive storm erupts. The terrified disciples wake him up, but Jesus criticizes their lack of faith before rebuking the weather. Everything stills. The storm is gone. The stunned disciples ask, "who is this man, that even the winds and the waves obey him?" It's a significant question. Who alone but God can wield power over the natural elements of this earth? The answer is a resounding, "No one!"

OVER ANIMALS

We grant God's sovereignty over inanimate objects like wind and water, but what about animals? Scripture teaches that God rules over His creatures, including the animals. Not a single sparrow will fall to the ground without the Lord's doing (Matthew 10:29).

In Genesis 6, Noah and his family will load onto an ark and be the surviving remnant of humanity after the great flood. God is also going to spare the beasts, birds, and livestock by having a pair of each kind, male and female, preserved on the ark. Have you ever wondered how Noah gathered all those animals? Have you ever stopped to consider what trying to capture and contain those animals required? Noah didn't wrangle these creatures. They came to the ark in twos because God sovereignly directed them.

In Genesis 22, Abraham takes Isaac, his son, to a mountaintop to sacrifice Isaac as God commanded. But just before committing the act, an angel of the LORD stops Abraham. When Abraham looks up, there's a ram caught in a thicket by his horns. Is this the unluckiest ram ever? Is this good luck for Abraham and Isaac? No. Abraham recognizes that the LORD delivered this provision. He told Isaac earlier that God would provide the sacrifice, and now He had (22:8). In fact, Abraham was so aware that God sent the ram that he names the place "The LORD will provide"

(22:14). God sent a ram to their location, and trapped it in a thicket. Then they made a sacrifice, provided by God. Luck wasn't involved.

Before Moses brought the Hebrews out of Egypt, the LORD sent plagues as a judgment against Pharaoh. He sent frogs, gnats, flies, and locusts to invade the land (Exodus 8-10). Even the livestock died. How did these living creatures suddenly invade Egypt? Why did all the frogs descend in mass upon the city? How did the flies, gnats, and locusts get the sudden urge to invade? Because they were under the sovereign command of God. God sent them.

OVER SUFFERING

I could continue showing God's sovereignty over things like Satan and demons, humans, and salvation, but space doesn't permit it. The purpose of our look at the sovereignty of God is learning to trust God through our pains. We want peace to fill our hearts, even when strife fills our lives. This happens only as we recognize God as sovereign over our suffering, and over our lives.

But does the sovereignty of God include our pain? Can we say that God is in control over trials and afflictions that come into our lives? How sovereign is God, really?

Those questions pervaded my mind. They led to the most important question: What does the Bible say about God's sovereignty over the affairs of our lives?

31

Your eyes saw my unformed substance; in your book were written, every one of them, the days that were formed for me, when as yet there was none of them. —
Psalm 139:16

Every day of our lives are written by God, in His book, before one day ever came to be. God saw our lives before we had a life. Where did He see it? In His own mind. He is author of our stories. We existed in the mind of God before we ever existed in time. And He wrote all the days of our lives in His book. He determined the length of our days, and the particulars of our experiences. That means our lives are not left to randomness or chance. God is sovereign over them.

This passage became key for me in learning to trust God's plan through Kaleb's sufferings. I remember driving over a bridge across the interstate a few months before Kaleb's kidney transplant. My mind raced as I thought about him getting a transplant to save his life. "Will we find a transplant?" "Can he survive the surgery?" "Will the transplant work?" "How long will this transplant endure, and what happens if it fails?" These thoughts scared me, but then the Holy Spirit brought Psalm 139:16 to mind.

Suddenly I remembered, "God is in control of Kaleb's life. He wrote all of Kaleb's days in His book. The first and last days are written. There's nothing anybody can do to add one day to his life, and there's nothing anybody can do to take one away. God is sovereign over his life."

My brewing anxiousness subsided as God's Word saturated my heart and mind. The reality of God's sovereignty reminds me there are no accidents with God. Kaleb's struggles had purpose. His pain had meaning. Our uncertainties were not uncertain for God. We had to trust God's plan.

HIS PLANS STAND

God's plans—including the ones He makes for our lives—succeed. The Bible testifies on this throughout its pages.

For the LORD of hosts has purposed, and who will annul it? His hand is stretched out, and who will turn it back? — Isaiah 14:27

The questions in this verse are rhetorical. The answers are assumed in the asking. Who can annul God's purposes or turn back His hand? Nobody. No one can annul God's plans. There's no power outside of God to cancel what He determines to do. Nobody can turn back His outstretched hand. The image here is of God's will in motion, His outstretched hand taking action. And nothing in the universe stops that hand when He's determined to act. He's sovereign.

I know that you can do all things, and that
no purpose of yours can be thwarted. — Job 42:2

Job suffered many losses. Afflictions had devastated his life and turned everything upside down. Satan was the secondary agent of those things, but God gave the permission. Job gripes to God, but the LORD puts a quick end to it. God speaks about his work creating everything that exists and then asks why Job's infinite knowledge wasn't available for use at the creation of the world (Job 40). Job backs down. He replies that he knows the LORD can do all things.

Nobody thwarts or hinders God's plans or purposes. When He acts, it's settled.

"Remember this and stand firm,
recall it to mind, you transgressors,
remember the former things of old;
for I am God, and there is no other;
I am God, and there is none like me,
declaring the end from the beginning
and from ancient times things not yet done,
saying, 'My counsel shall stand,
and I will accomplish all my purpose,'
calling a bird of prey from the east,
the man of my counsel from a far country.
I have spoken, and I will bring it to pass;
I have purposed, and I will do it. — Isaiah 46:8-11

This passage is breathtaking. God declares the end from the beginning. He declares it, not predicts it. He determines it, not guesses it. He speaks from ancient times things not yet done. These are His counsels and decrees, and He has determined that His counsels will stand, and His purposes be accomplished. When God speaks and purposes, it's done.

Some people stumble over this doctrine because they conclude God's sovereignty means we're robots that don't make choices. Arguments from philosophy instead of Scripture can lead you to that conclusion. But when you read the Bible, there are two truths that are presented as compatible with one another: (1) God is sovereign over everything that happens; (2) we make real choices, with real consequences, and God holds us accountable for them. We don't have to untangle how it all works, but we must believe it.

Some folks hesitate to embrace God's sovereignty because they don't see how sin and evil fit in. I get it. It's not easy to get your mind around. And while explaining different possibilities is not the focus of this book, it's important to note that the Bible isn't afraid to address the subject.

I form light and create darkness; I make well-being and create calamity; I am the LORD, who does all these things. — Isaiah 45:7

The word "calamity" in this verse is the Hebrew verb for "evil" (רַע – ra'). Why avoid saying evil in the translation? Bible translators modify it because it's a troublesome word for many to associate with God. Most people haven't thought about God's relationship to evil and suffering. We assume evil is bad—and it is —so we can assume God can't have any part to play in it. But Lamentations 3:37-38 is another example of Scripture supporting God's sovereignty over it all: "Who has spoken and it came to pass, unless the LORD has commanded it? Is it not from the mouth of the Most High that good and bad come?"

Most people avoid wrestling through these ideas, but I've addressed it because these are natural questions that arise on this subject. And it's relevant as you reflect on the sovereignty of God over your circumstances. When tragedy, sorrow, and afflictions surround our lives, we must ask: Where is God in this? Does He sit back passively watching, wishing these things didn't happen? Or are they included in His ultimate plans for our lives, and the world? The answer we must give from Scripture is that whether God plans or permits our suffering, He is sovereign over it. If we are enduring it, it isn't by fate or chance. God is sovereign even over our pain.

Here's another passage that aides our understanding of Scripture on this question.

But, though He cause grief, He will have compassion according to the abundance of His steadfast love; for He does not afflict from His heart or grieve the children of men. — Lamentations 3:32-33

God doesn't afflict for affliction's sake. He may cause grief, but not because He has an appetite for toying with us. Pain is not His goal. We're not the center of a cosmic game He's playing. He doesn't purpose evil for evil's sake.

As a father, I know when to protect my girls from pain, and when it is okay to let them experience it. They need to experience things that hurt. They need to learn how to cope with disappointment. However, as a wise father, I know when to allow those experiences and when to protect them from unnecessary pain.

Make no mistake, our transcendent God is qualified to decree good and evil without His holiness and goodness being contaminated.

Attempts to dissect these things confuse even the smartest people. And admittedly, much of it is bound up with faith and mystery (Job 40:1-5; Deuteronomy 29:29; Ephesians 1:9; 3:1-13). Sometimes using affirmations and denials is the most helpful approach.

We affirm God ordains all that comes to pass. We deny He commits any evil. We affirm nothing comes to pass outside His ultimate will. We deny God can commit sin. We affirm no suffering can happen apart from God willing it. We deny suffering is pointless.

This raises lots of questions, and that's okay.[1] But nothing I've asserted is smuggled in from outside Scripture. These are God's own words.

WRESTLE WITH THESE THINGS

This truth was huge for me to contemplate, given Kaleb's struggles. For years I dove into Scripture, studying commentaries, reading books, and working through the philosophical ideas. I also worked through my heart's reaction to these truths. Nobody ever sat me down and taught me these things. I learned them in the middle of deep pain, Bible in hand, in the heat of the fiery furnace.

Scripture showed me that God ruled over all of Kaleb's trials. This included the surgical mistake, having a stroke, and breathing his last breath. Knowing God was sovereign became my only comfort.

There was no comfort in believing God wanted to stop it, but couldn't. There was no relief in believing God didn't plan it, but only allowed it.

If He could have stopped Kaleb's surgical mistake or healed his sick body, but didn't, then He willed not to do it. Attempts to exonerate God from willing an event to happen are impossible unless we deny God's very nature as God. No, I reached the place where I

---

[1] A good book for deeper study on this subject is *What About Evil? A Defense of God's Sovereign Glory* by Scott Christensen

believed and embraced Scripture's teaching about God's purposeful directing of the entire universe, from beginning to end, including the difficulties.

KYRA'S QUESTION

My youngest daughter, Kyra, had just turned 6 years old when Kaleb died. More than a year later, she traveled with me to an event I spoke at in Melbourne, Florida. At the end of my first session, I brought up Kaleb's death. And as I spoke, I saw Kyra in the crowd crying. It broke my heart. A sweet lady saw her and sat beside Kyra to console her while I finished.

We left the church. Tears still rolled down her cheeks. We hadn't eaten dinner, so we made our way to a restaurant.

I put my hand on her lap as we drove, "Are you okay, sweetie?"

"I miss Kaleb."

"Me too, sweetheart."

"I don't understand," as tears trickled down her face, "why doesn't God just make it all better?"

The complexity of the question stunned me. She was only seven and a half years old. Her heart understood the implications of God's sovereign power over a world where her brother dies. But her question wasn't over.

"Why didn't God create the world the way Heaven will be, where no sin and bad stuff happen?"

She cried as she asked this question. My daughter

was asking something that has consumed philosophers and theologians for thousands of years. It's a question every Christian should ask and answer. And yet the question terrified me. "Oh God, don't let her little heart get hard toward you," I prayed.

I attempted to explain my answer as best as I could to her.

"I understand your question, and it is a great question, sweetheart. God could have created a different world, like the one we'll see when Jesus comes back. But He didn't. That means there's something about how God created our world, where even sin, pain, and death, show how wonderful He is —in a way that wouldn't be seen without those things."

That's my answer. I believe it's 100% true. I had one hand on the wheel and one on Kyra's knee, squeezing both as I reminded her that we must seek Jesus for our help and comfort. God promises one day that kind of world will be ours. One day we will hug Kaleb again. All because of Jesus.

This leaves us with trusting Him. I trust God is in complete control, including my life. But this isn't the only attribute we must embrace in order to find peace in our trials. If this attribute stood alone, God could be impersonal and cruel. He could be a sovereign fool, or a tyrant. And that's why we must also understand the next attribute we're examining—God's wisdom.

Discussion Questions

1. Describe in your own words what you think it means for God to be completely sovereign.

2. Read the following Scriptures and discuss the different ways and aspects that they describe God's sovereignty: 1 Chronicles 29:11-12, Psalm 139:16, Isaiah 14:27, Job 42:2, Proverbs 16:9, Proverbs 19:21.

3. What are the biggest difficulties that come with believing or comprehending God's sovereignty?

4. Is it easy or difficult for you to be in charge? Not in charge? Give an example of how/where you struggle with this, especially when it comes to letting God be in charge.

5. What do you think is most significant in John 10:17-18 to your understanding of God's sovereignty? What difference would it make if Christ's death were not the plan and initiative of the Godhead?

6. In light of God's sovereignty, discuss the following passages and how they can bring comfort to you in times of trial and suffering: Ephesians 4:10, Philippians 4:6-7, John 14:27, Jeremiah 29:11, Psalm 23:4.

4

THE WISDOM OF GOD

As a teenager, I thought my parents were dumb. I admit it. I believed their rules were arbitrary and only intent on squelching my enjoyment of life. When I say "dumb," I'm not speaking of intellectual shortcomings. I mean simple and pointless. Their rules of "dos and don'ts" didn't appear to have brains behind them.

Now that I'm older, and have kids myself, I realize they weren't as dimwitted as I first suspected; in fact, I now recognize there was wisdom in their rules and ways. But I was too immature to understand it. What appeared foolish was actually wise, but I couldn't see the wisdom because I was a fool. Proverbs 23:9 explains my problem, "Do not speak in the hearing of a fool, for he will despise the good sense of your words."

As we approach the wisdom of God, we come

upon a new mountain to climb. The wisdom of God is higher than our capacity to scale it. We can seek it, get glimpses of it, and trust it, but we cannot exhaust it. Our minds can't comprehend it. And if we're not careful, we can end up acting like I did as a teenager: unable to see the wisdom of God's ways, and concluding it must be lacking.

GOD'S WISDOM

The wisdom of God means that God always chooses the best purposes and the best means for achieving those purposes. He always decides what's best according to His perspective, not ours. God's infinite wisdom guides His eternal plans. The wisdom of God permeates His creation in the ordering, guidance, and government of all things in it. Because wisdom informs His decisions and decrees, He never has regrets.[2] He never utters "oops." He never says, "I made a poor decision" or "I made a mistake."

The reason God always chooses the best is because He has inexhaustible knowledge. God knows all things. There are no secrets. There's no subject in the universe where He lacks understanding. He doesn't need to brush up on the facts. God's knowledge includes our thoughts, words, and activities. He knows every turn

---

[2] See John Piper's podcast at DesiringGod.org entitled: "Why Does God Regret and Repent in the Bible?" See also Kevin DeYoung's article at The Gospel Coalition entitled: "Does God Have Regret?"

of the airplane propeller, angles of each blade of grass as the wind blows, the speed of every car driving down the road, and the tire pressure of each tire— simultaneously, every second, forever. He always knows the path that accomplishes his twin purposes of bringing glory to His name and bringing joy and flourishing to His people. His wisdom always guides it.

Many facets of God's wisdom are a mystery. The wisdom of God is not something we can fully comprehend or understand. Some things God does according to His wisdom won't look wise to us. But God reminds us in Isaiah 55:8-9, "For my thoughts are not your thoughts, neither are your ways my ways, declares the LORD. For as the heavens are higher than the earth, so are my ways higher than your ways and my thoughts than your thoughts."

God says His thoughts and our thoughts are worlds apart. We get glimpses, but it shouldn't shock us that we don't fathom or understand the wisdom in something God ordains.

Oh, the depth of the riches and wisdom and knowledge of God! How unsearchable are his judgments and how inscrutable his ways! "For who has known the mind of the Lord, or who has been his counselor?" "Or who has given a gift to him that he might be repaid?" For from him and through him and to him are all things. To him be glory forever. Amen. — Romans 11:33-36

Human exploration will never plumb the depths of the wisdom of God. We'll put a man at the edge of the universe before we reach the depths of God's wisdom. His judgments and ways are inscrutable, meaning, impossible to understand and interpret. God's incomprehensibility, His otherness, is so great that it prevents us from judging or even assessing His inscrutable plans. We are incapable of affirming His plans based on our understanding of His decrees. It leaves us only to trust Him. We must rely on Scripture's testimony that God always acts according to the counsel of His will (Ephesians 1:11). God's plans are not arbitrary or half-baked. The implication for us: God's will is wise and best, even when our minds don't grasp how.

BRINGING IT TOGETHER

All of God's attributes stay in continuous action. He never switches from one to another. His sovereignty and wisdom operate alongside His holiness and goodness. This cancels charges of evil against Him. And He doesn't change. He's the same yesterday, today, and forever (Hebrews 13:8).

What if God only kept one of these attributes without the others? If God were sovereign, but lacked wisdom, He would possess all power and authority, but would also be capable of foolish and reckless decisions. If He were wise, but not sovereign, He would know the best plan, but lack the power to execute it.

There's great clarity in seeing the sovereignty and wisdom of God held together. We learn that nothing happens by chance, or passes outside God's plans. Everything filters through His wisdom. This helps weary sufferers to remember that our pains and afflictions are not pointless. Trials are hard enough, but thinking they are without purpose is even harder.

NEVERTHELESS

I want to drive these truths into our hearts. These are not intellectual exercises for theology nerds, they're the foundation under our feet for actual life. These realities comfort us that nothing is random. Nothing happens by chance. We're not at the mercy of other people's whims or mistakes. Everything God decrees and brings to pass stems from His wisdom, which consoles us that God knows best. His plans bring blessing to His people. God works all things for the good of His people, who are called according to His purpose (Romans 8:28).

How do you react when your expectations of God's actions differ from His actual actions? What's your response when there's a massive gap between your preferred future versus the one He brings? When Job complains about his afflictions, the essence of God's answer to Job was, "I am God, and you are not."

The response that takes us toward trusting God is humble submission. Elisabeth Elliot taught about how to respond to suffering. In her book, *Suffering is Never for Nothing*, she says we should open our hands to receive whatever God gives us, including suffering. "Thank you, Lord" is our reply. We may not understand or like it. We may hurt. It may crash our life dreams or keep us in a painful situation, but we submit to God's will.

The prophet Eli's response when he discovered God was going to strike down his two sons (1 Samuel 3:18) was, "It is the LORD. Let him do what seems good to Him." He displayed humble submission. I'm sure his heart broke, and tears filled his eyes as Samuel relayed to him the message God revealed. But he submitted. He trusted the Lord.

Our response reveals a great deal about us. How we react to what God does reveals whether we have a man-centered view of the world or a God-centered view. It shows whether we think God exists for our purposes, or we exist for God's purposes.

Jesus, our Savior and King, models humble submission. In the Garden of Gethsemane, Jesus was hours from facing the wrath of God on the cross for our sin. Jesus experienced an eternity in Hell during those three hours at Calvary, and He did that so His people wouldn't have to face Hell for even a second. But before the cross, He prayed in Matthew 26:39, "My Father, if it be possible, let this cup pass from me; nevertheless, not as I will, but as you will."

Jesus, the Lamb of God, saw the cost for sin's

atonement, and prayed the Father might offer another way. No other way came. He could only walk through one door to accomplish His task. And His soul was in anguish.

This is the tension I'm describing in this chapter: a life of faith confronts us with trusting in God's sovereign plan and wisdom, while living in the anguish, pain, and suffering we encounter. What did Jesus do, when the sovereign and wise plan of the Father involved drinking the cup instead of letting it pass? He said, "Nevertheless, not my will, but your will be done." Humble submission to the sovereignty and wisdom of God.

This is our battle. When it's established in our minds and hearts that God is sovereign and wise, and we face things we wish were different, do we humbly submit? Are we "nevertheless" people? Can we repeat with Eli, "It is the LORD. Let Him do what seems good to him."?

YOUR STORMS

When doctors give a terminal cancer diagnosis, and you can't understand why this would be God's plan, and your wisdom believes another way would be better, pray, "God, I don't want to leave people I love, but I submit to You."

When your marriage struggles make you question how you can stay, and walking away seems to promise happiness, but you have no biblical grounds for divorce, pray, "Lord, I'm not happy and want to leave, nevertheless, I trust You."

When you're facing infertility as a couple, and can't understand why God doesn't give you a child when you'd be such good parents, pray, "You know we want children, and it feels like our lives are incomplete, nevertheless, Lord, Your will be done."

When you struggle with sexual desires outside of the Bible's boundaries, and the culture is telling you it's okay to fulfill those desires, pray, "Everyone is telling me to live my truth and pursue a sexually fulfilled life, but nevertheless, Lord, I trust Your plan for me."

When a child, sibling, friend, or family member unexpectedly dies, pray, "I don't want to live without this person in my life, or experience the pain of grief and sorrow, but Your plans are wiser than mine."

When God hasn't brought a husband or wife into your life yet, pray, "You see the desires of my heart, but nevertheless, Lord, I submit to Your will."

When God calls you to a task or responsibility, but you feel unworthy and unprepared, pray, "I'm not sure I'm ready or good enough to do this, but, Lord, Your will be done."

When crippling anxiety, depression, or physical ailments have no end in sight, pray, "My desire is to live free of this, but I trust You."

PRAYERFUL SURRENDER

There are so many more examples I could give. It's

unending. When the sovereignty and wisdom of God seeps into our hearts, and brings us to humble submission to His will and plan for us, our trust in the LORD grows. How do we trust the LORD? Our hearts rest in the One who is sovereign and wise in everything that happens. Tim Keller once said, "If we knew what God knows, we would ask exactly for what He gives." Why is that? Because we would see and understand the wisdom and goodness of it.

Our prayers may be, "I don't understand, Lord; I don't get it. I don't see what purpose You have in this!" And that's okay, the Lord can handle our honesty, and He knows the cries of our hearts. But rather than ending there, we should continue the prayer, "But I trust you, Lord. If you have allowed, permitted, or planned it, I trust You. You are wiser than me. Your plans surpass mine. Help me not to lean on my understanding. Give me rest and peace in Your sovereign will."

That's the prayer of faith. That is the heart learning to trust in the LORD.

Discussion Questions

1. Describe in your own words what you think it means for God to be completely wise.

2. Read the following Scriptures and discuss how they describe God's wisdom: Isaiah 55:8-9, Romans 11:33-36, Isaiah 40:28, 1 Corinthians 1:25.

3. What are the biggest difficulties that come with believing or comprehending God's wisdom?

4. Why is trusting God's wisdom vital for learning to trust Him with the things we experience and endure in this life?

5. What is the most difficult part of living our lives like Eli (who said, "It is the LORD. Let him do what seems good to him.") or Jesus (when he said, "Nevertheless, your will, not my will, be done.")? Why is humble submission not our default way of handling trials when they come?

6. What are ways we can grow in our understanding God's wisdom so that we are more prone to trust Him through suffering and sorrow?

5

THE LOVE OF GOD

Don't skip this chapter. If you're anything like me, moving past this chapter is a real temptation. The moment you read the chapter title, you concluded, "I know God is love. I can move on." But I hope you will see the love of God is significant to our learning to trust Him through our trials. The complexity of the subject goes beyond the simplifications the culture trots out for consumption.

When we talk about the love of God, we are talking about God's giving of Himself for the benefit of others. God's nature is to give Himself away to others, to bring about blessing and goodness to them. The nature of God is love. It's His essence, even before creating the world. Our Triune God—Father, Son, and Holy Spirit—experiences love between each member of the Godhead without needing to create a world or anything else in order to express that love. It's important to grasp this point: God doesn't need us in order to exercise His attribute of love. He didn't need to create the world in order to fulfill His desire to love. God is love (1 John 4:8).

Imagine a couple with three biological children deciding to adopt a child. They're not adopting because they're lacking love or have no way of expressing their parental love, it's because they desire to give the love they have to another, to one who hasn't experienced it. That's what the Triune God does in giving us His love. He doesn't create us because He needs us to satisfy His desire to love. He created us because of His desire to share the love that the Godhead has known for eternity (1 John 1:2-3).

TWO DITCHES

To talk about the love of God, we need to define and distinguish what we mean. The love of God is the most popular attribute of God espoused by our culture. It's often used as a defensive weapon against charges of sin and unrighteousness. Christians and non-Christians appeal to God's love as a justification for many things. People appeal to the love of God as a counter argument when anyone implies God hates sin and that we should repent from it. "Yeah, but God is love" is the common refrain. When people want you to quit talking about their sin, they appeal to the love of God, as if that nullifies everything else.

God is love. But our culture today misunderstands the love of God. In fact, many Christians get it wrong too. Many speak about God's love as is if He dotes on us because we're so special. This understanding of God's love leaves us unchanged. It affirms us in our sins. So I don't love the statement, "He loves us just the way we are." I get the intention, but it needs a lot of qualification. "God loves us" has become synonymous with "God approves of my behavior" even when God plainly states in Scripture that He abhors that behavior. No, God loves us as we are—showing it through the sacrifice of Christ for us (Romans 5:8)—but because He loves us, He changes us. Encountering God's love, and the biblical understanding of the love of God, transforms our lives.

When it comes to this subject, there are two ditches people usually fall into. The first ditch sees God's love as an airy, fluffy, and feel-good thing. The second ditch dislikes talking about the love of God altogether because it seems icky, weak, and soft. This group would rather talk about the wrath of God. In my experience, women drift toward the first ditch, and men drift toward the second ditch. But both ditches are wrong. And it is the path between the ditches that unveils the grandeur of God's love. This path recognizes there is beauty, substance, and weightiness to the love of God.

LOVE FOR ALL

God loves everyone. This is a true biblical

statement. This is the 30,000 ft. aerial view of God's love. Scripture testifies to this.

> *For he makes his sun rise on the evil and on the good, and sends rain on the just and on the unjust.* — *Matthew 5:45*

God displays His love to the world every second. He gives even those who curse and hate Him breath in their lungs, laughter and full bellies, and marriages and children. These are undeserved gifts from the Lord. All these common graces are evidences of His love. It is a love given away every day in simple pleasures and unfathomable blessings, regardless of whether the individual reciprocates that love. We can look any person in the eye and say with conviction and confidence, "God loves you." And there is an abundance of evidence behind our claim.

LOVE FOR THE SHEEP

While God loves every person, we can add with confidence that He loves His people differently. He loves the church, His bride, differently (Ephesians 5:25-33). There is a particular love God has for His sheep that differs from His love for the unrepentant and rebellious sinner. God's love doesn't fluctuate up and down, but He gives His sheep the grace to experience deeper dimensions and portions of His love. God's particular love for His people differs from His general love that all people experience.

We understand this at a subconscious level already. When I tell the church I pastor "I love you," they never confuse that love for being the same as the love I have for my wife. When I tell a brother or sister in Christ, "I love you," they don't equate that to the same love I have for my children. One isn't more real or genuine than the other, but they are different.

The same is true for God's love. He loves everyone. But He loves His people with a particular love that is distinctive. God's love for His people begins in eternity, not in time.

Blessed be the God and Father of our Lord Jesus Christ, who has blessed us in Christ with every spiritual blessing in the heavenly places, even as he chose us in him before the foundation of the world, that we should be holy and blameless before him. In love he predestined us for adoption to himself as sons through Jesus Christ, according to the purpose of his will, to the praise of his glorious grace, with which he has blessed us in the Beloved. — Ephesians 1:3-6

Before we were even born, God the Father chose us, in Christ, that we should be holy and blameless before Him. What drove Him to give us this destiny? Love. His love for us directed His adoption of us into

His family. This was all—as we've already studied—according to the purpose of His will. This was a part of His grand plan from the beginning—as Paul says in Ephesians 1:4, "before the foundation of the world."

God loved us before we were born. This isn't a response to our loving Him, but His loving us. And it is displayed through the sacrificial death of His Son.

In this is love, not that we have loved God but that he loved us and sent his Son to be the propitiation for our sins. — 1 John 4:10

At the cross, Jesus became a propitiation for our sins. That means He became a sacrifice that bore the wrath of God, and in doing so, diverted that wrath off of us. The love of the Father is that He sent His Son in order that Jesus might save us and make us His own. The love of the Son is that He came and bore our sin at the cross, to bring us back to God (1 Peter 3:18). And the Holy Spirit's love is seen as He applies the work of Christ to our hearts by opening our eyes to the gospel, enabling us to respond by faith (John 3:3).

In Christ, you are loved with a particular love. And that love is never shelved, ignored, or forgotten in God's plans for you.

GIVER OF ALL THINGS

Here's a question for you to consider: Does the

Father love us because Christ died for us? Or did Christ die for us because the Father loves us? If the Father loves us only because Jesus died for us, then the Father's love is conditional. How so? Well, it required Christ's death to make Him love us. But if Christ died because the Father already loved us, then that shows God's love for us preexisted our salvation. In fact, it shows us that God's love is why Jesus came into the world and died a sacrificial death. His death didn't create that love for us; it was the demonstration of that love. And this is indeed what the Scriptures teach us.

Not only that, but the God who purchased us from the dead and saved our souls isn't finished with us. He redeemed us from sin and death for a reason.

He who did not spare his own Son but gave him up for us all, how will he not also with him graciously give us all things? — Romans 8:32

Will God provide and care for us in the small things? Will He tend to the needs of His adopted and rescued children? Yes! In fact, nothing will separate us from the love of God in Christ (Romans 8:38). Nothing. He lavishes it on us forever.

If we belong to Christ, there's nothing we can do to make God love us more, and there is nothing we can do for Him to love us less. Why? Because His love is unconditional. We don't earn it, so we can't lose it. If we are in Christ, then God has loved us with the fullness of His love, and we will not lose it. He may discipline us for our sin and disobedience, but that is not withholding His love for us. It's the opposite. God disciplines those whom He loves (Hebrews 12:6).

Many Christians live each day thinking the love of God functions like a bank account. It goes up when you make positive contributions and behave well, and they think it depletes when they mess up, sin, and have bad days. Because our default mode is conditional love, we assume God's love fluctuates like a scale based on how good our day went.

It doesn't.

God is pleased with His people because of the finished work of His Son. He delights in His people, because the righteousness of Christ covers them.

TRIALS AND GOD'S LOVE

In Journey Worship Co.'s song "With All My Heart," the second verse says, "Your love is rich and deep, it's lavished on Your sheep, assuring me Your will is always good." This idea of God's particular love for His people breeds confidence when troubles and trials come. When we don't understand God's plan, we can rely on what we know is true: God loves us.

For me, since losing Kaleb, I constantly go back to the truth that God, in His sovereignty and wisdom, knows what is best. He has intentions and designs in all His plans. I remember His particular love for me, for Katrina and the girls, and for Kaleb. His plans were never abstract or distant from His intimate, personal love for us. We are His children. This brings the sovereignty and wisdom of God, which can seem impersonal and distant, up close and personal. He never forms His sovereign and wise plans detached from His love. This helps me even when I don't understand His plans.

Oh, child of God, do you sense His love for you today? Don't let the weight of sins, struggles, and suffering deceive your heart. Listen to Paul's prayer for the church in Ephesus, and to us, as he prays that we:

may have strength to comprehend with all the saints what is the breadth and length and height and depth, and to know the love of Christ that surpasses knowledge, that you may be filled with all the fullness of God. — Ephesians 3:18-19

Paul asks God to provide us the strength to comprehend with other believers the great breadth, length, height, and depth of the love of God and to know this love of Christ that surpasses knowledge. He is praying that we would comprehend something that surpasses knowledge! It's like saying, "I wish you had the power to count the grains of sand, which are too many to count."

Why desire such a thing?

Because in trying to comprehend its complexity, the grandeur and greatness of the thing increases, even if we only grow in increments of understanding. The more of God's incomprehensible love we comprehend, the more we stand in awe and wonder. When we start to see it, it changes us, even if we only get glimpses.

God's unbreakable pleasure with us stands secure by the finished work of Jesus on our behalf. There is no need to earn approval. In Christ, we have the full approval of God. There's nothing that can make God love us more, and there's nothing that can make God love us less. And the One who loves us with this great incalculable love, is the One who sovereignly and wisely created the purposes and plans for our lives.

We are not a statistic to God. We are not one face in a sea of faces to Him. He knows every hair on our heads, including its color and length, down to the fractions of an inch. At all times we have access to Him through Christ. He hears our internal whispers and cries.

The All-Knowing, All-Seeing God who made us, loves us. Won't you trust Him? Won't you submit yourself to His sovereign and wise plans? Won't you cling to His promises for you amid your troubles instead of letting fear and worry, bitterness and regret, rule your life?

Turn to Him today. Trust in the LORD with all

your heart and do not lean on your own understanding. In all your ways acknowledge Him, and He will make straight your paths.

Discussion Questions

1. How is the love of God as described in Scripture different from the way the world defines it? (1 John 4:10, 1 John 3:1, Ephesians 2:4-5, Romans 5:8, Romans 8:35-39) Why is it important to understand the difference?

2. When the world talks about God's love it is a typically in conjunction with excusing away sinful practices that God condemns in Scripture. Why is that? Why is the love of God used this way so frequently by the world?

3. In what ways can we distinguish God's love for all people from God's love for His bride, the church?

4. What makes God's love for us personally so powerful in learning to trust God through our trials and tribulations?

5. Discuss why it's important to understand that if I am in Christ I can't do anything to make God love me any more than He does or make Him love me any less than He does.

6. When we are in the middle of difficulties and storms, what effect does the love of God have in helping our hearts be at rest and peace?

6

THE FAITHFULNESS OF GOD

Around my house we have a fun way of responding when something good happens. If Katrina is looking for the pizza cutter and can't find it, and she's digging through kitchen drawers in search of it, and finally comes across it, she may say, "Look at God! Won't He do it?!" And the reply I'll give is, "He said He would!" Or if I'm opening the mail and we have a refund check from our insurance company in there, I may hold it up and say, "Look at God!" Katrina responds, "Won't He do it?" And I'll say, "Said He would!"

This style of banter in the Reed house is a fun way we respond when unexpected good happens, if they're silly things. But the heart of what we're saying is that God is faithful. "Won't He do it?" "He said He would." That last statement is the key to understanding God's faithfulness.

The previous three chapters have centered on God's sovereignty, wisdom, and love. In this chapter we're locking-in on God's commitment to always do what He says He'll do. God always fulfills His promises. That's what it means that God is faithful. Understanding this attribute is vital to our quest to trust God with all our hearts.

TRACK RECORD

Have you ever worked with someone who agreed to projects or tasks, but never accomplished them? Perhaps their intentions were pure, and their desires genuine, but they just never came through. I've known several people like that in my years of leadership. They had great intentions, and poor execution. They overpromised and under-delivered. As a leader, or even someone on a team with this kind of person, it's super frustrating. It leads to distrust. You can't count on that kind of person.

But God is not like that.

What God says He will do, He will do. He follows through. The Lord is dependable to accomplish His promises. This is not something we assert without evidence, nor something based on opinion. The Bible contains the historical record of God's dealings with humanity, and in it, we see amazing promises God gives and fulfills.

God promised to preserve Noah and his family from the Great Flood (Genesis 6:18). The sin and corruption of man had reached a boiling point. The LORD was bringing judgment upon the earth. He instructed Noah to build the ark, and He promised to spare Noah and pairs of all living creatures. And everything God promised, He fulfilled. The flood came. Destruction ensued. But God spared Noah and his family, including beasts and creatures that creep on the ground. He kept His Word.

A man named Abram (later renamed Abraham) received a promise from God (Genesis 12:1-3). The LORD told him to leave his homeland and go where God led him. There the LORD would establish Abram into a great nation. Abram and Sarah were childless, but God promised descendants as countless as the stars. And God fulfilled His promise. Abraham had Isaac. Isaac had Jacob. And Jacob had twelve sons that would make up the twelve tribes of Israel.

The LORD instructed Moses to lead the Israelites out of Egyptian captivity. Moses fretted over his lack of skills for public speaking. But God continued telling Moses that He would show His power through him. And God did. Through the plagues and the hardening of Pharaoh's heart, Moses was able to lead the Israelites from Egypt by God's might. The LORD fulfilled His promise.

And in doing so, God also fulfilled His promise to Abraham. When Israel sought refuge in Egypt during the life of Joseph (Abraham's great-grandson), they numbered 70 people. Note that number again. Not 7,000. Not 70,000. Only 70 people. But when Moses led them out, there were 600,000 men, not counting women and children (Exodus 12:37). God fulfilled His promise.

God promised David victory over foreign armies, and a kingdom whose throne would never be vacant belonging to his descendants (1 Chronicles 17:11-14). David defeated armies in battle, not because of his strength, but because of the LORD'S favor. Israel routed stronger armies because the LORD fulfilled His promise to David. And David's kingdom still has no end. After David came Solomon, and after him, mostly terrible kings. But one day, in the city of David, a mother's birth pangs and screams of labor gave way to a joyous time of celebration and worship. Born to young Mary was a child who would sit on David's throne, not for a lifetime, but for an eternity. Jesus, the Messiah and King, is the fulfillment of God's promise to David. And He fulfilled it, because God is faithful to His promises.

HE CAN'T HELP IT

My friend, Jeff, has a unique personality. He's always got a joke. He's rarely serious. The consistency of his character and personality over many years makes it difficult to know when he's not joking. People who know him expect a punchline. Right when we think he's having a serious moment, he delivers the one-liner. He can't help himself. That's who he is.

God's faithfulness to His Word and promises is who He is. In a sense, He can't help Himself. It's intrinsic to His nature to follow through on what He says.

> *if we are faithless, he remains faithful—for he*
> *cannot deny himself.* — 2 Timothy 2:13

Our confidence in God's promises stems from the confidence we have in His character. God never breaks His Word. He gives promises through His Word that should give life to His people. God speaks in Scripture to reveal Himself, to teach us about who we are, to show us His ways, and to tell us about the future He intends to bring. Those things are all true because God reveals them. The God who said, "Let there be light" accomplishes everything He declares.

As Christians, this is vital for us to cling to. We are to live in light of the promises of God. We seek to live trusting in the LORD, but to do that requires knowing who He is, and letting it saturate our hearts and minds. The promises He gives us in this life are ours to take hold of. And those promises amid our trials, suffering, and pain stabilize us to press forward with trust.

PROMISES TO HOLD

One of the most important promises of Scripture we cling to as Christians is our forgiveness of sins through the finished work of Jesus. Through faith in Jesus—both his death on the cross for our sins and his resurrection from the dead—we are saved. God

reconciles us to Himself, and we become His adopted
children, heirs with eternal and imperishable
inheritance.

*If we confess our sins, he is faithful and just to
forgive us our sins and to cleanse us from all
unrighteousness.* — 1 John 1:9

*In him we have redemption through his blood, the
forgiveness of our trespasses, according to the riches of his
grace.* — Ephesians 1:7

God's children, adopted by grace, have this
incredible promise to comfort us: He is always with us.
We're never alone. He is closer than any of us imagine
or perceive. This promise is one we cling to as we
endure the rough waters of life.

*fear not, for I am with you; be not dismayed, for I
am your God; I will strengthen you, I will help you, I will
uphold you with my righteous right hand.* — Isaiah
41:10

*And behold, I am with you always, to the end of
the age.* — Matthew 28:20

*The LORD is near to the brokenhearted and saves
the crushed in spirit.* — Psalm 34:18

As Christians, the Lord never promises us He will prevent us from suffering trials. In fact, we are told to expect them (1 Peter 4:12). But the promise God gives us is that His sustaining grace will keep us in our trials. His power, not ours, will hold us up.

But he said to me, "My grace is sufficient for you, for my power is made perfect in weakness." Therefore I will boast all the more gladly of my weaknesses, so that the power of Christ may rest upon me. — 2 Corinthians 12:9

God is our refuge and strength, a very present help in trouble. — Psalm 46:1

Pain and sorrows are a reality we must all acknowledge. Any illusions that being a Christian exempts us from pain is wishful thinking, not Scripture. The Lord does not shelter us from trials, in fact, God uses them to mature and sanctify us (James 1:3-4). But God promises even more. He assures us of a future beyond our trials that anchors us to endure the afflictions of this world. Heaven awaits us.

In my Father's house are many rooms. If it were not so, would I have told you that I go to prepare a place for you? — John 14:2

Truly, truly, I say to you, whoever hears my word and believes him who sent me has eternal life. He does not come into judgment, but has passed from death to life. — *John 5:24*

If we belong to Christ, then we have the promise of eternal life. Jesus purchased our future, and our first day in Heaven will surpass every moment of pain.

For I consider that the sufferings of this present time are not worth comparing with the glory that is to be revealed to us. — *Romans 8:18*

So we do not lose heart. Though our outer self is wasting away, our inner self is being renewed day by day. For this light momentary affliction is preparing for us an eternal weight of glory beyond all comparison — *2 Corinthians 4:16-17*

And I heard a loud voice from the throne saying, "Behold, the dwelling place of God is with man. He will dwell with them, and they will be his people, and God himself will be with them as their God. He will wipe away every tear from their eyes, and death shall be no more, neither shall there be mourning, nor crying, nor pain anymore, for the former things have passed away." — *Revelation 21:3-4*

GLORIOUS PROMISES

The promises of God are life-giving. But they change our lives when we not only believe them, but live fueled by them. These promises supply power in our lives because the One making them keeps them. He writes them in sharpie, not pencil. They are as good as accomplished, because He who spoke them never lies. He keeps His Word. He is faithful. And He doesn't tie His faithfulness to our desires.

God's faithfulness isn't dependent upon whether we got what we wanted, or whether God adopted our plans. He is faithful to everything in His Word. That's the measure of God's faithfulness. We don't judge God's faithfulness by how often He fulfills our wants but His commitment to do what He says.

Trusting in the LORD with all of our heart requires trusting in the LORD. We have to know who He is. That's why we've studied the attributes of His sovereignty, wisdom, love, and faithfulness. So how do these truths tie together in such a way that fosters trust in God? How does knowing these attributes keep us from leaning on our own understanding? Those questions are where we now turn.

Discussion Questions

1. What does it mean when we say God is faithful?

2. How is it possible that we could errantly judge God's faithfulness by whether we got the results or outcomes we want in life?

3. Why is it better that God's faithfulness is tied to His promises and His Word instead of our desires?

4. How does the faithfulness of God serve to help us as we endure afflictions and troubles in life? What practical ways does God's faithfulness sustain us?

5. What are some of the promises of God that we cling to daily that it's vital God is faithful to keep?

6. Is there a promise of Scripture you need to cling to right now in light of things you are facing?

7

ONCE UPON A TIME

Have you ever noticed that humans are storytellers? It's one thing that separates us from all other created things. Yes, we are rational, but at an even deeper level we are storytellers. No other creature tells stories— they communicate in different ways—but they don't tell stories. We tell each other stories, but we're also constantly telling ourselves a story. We fill in the gaps with stories when we lack information. We interpret our lives through stories.

"The reason I don't get asked to help is because nobody likes me."

"Of course I'm not married yet because people think I'm ugly."

"My parents' divorce is probably my fault."

"He hasn't answered my texts because he's doing something he shouldn't be doing."

"My chest hurts when I move a certain way; it's something bad."

"It doesn't matter if I pray; nothing is going to change."

"There's no use in looking elsewhere; I'll never find a better job."

"They didn't follow me back on social media; I knew they didn't like me."

"We haven't had kids because God is punishing us for our past."

"What's the use of opening up and risking myself to hurt; you can't trust people."

"I'm the only single one in my friend group; I'm never going to find someone."

These examples are snapshots of the stories we tell ourselves every day. It's important to talk about this because the stories we tell ourselves can rule our emotional lives. Our views form through the stories we tell ourselves. And those stories affect our hearts, our hope, and our peace. Our minds construct elaborate stories and scenarios of things that haven't happened yet, and these stories end up having an actual effect on our emotions.

NIGHTIME IMAGINATIONS

I remember having trouble sleeping as a boy because I was afraid people were about to break into our house. Even as my parents sat in the living room with the television blaring, I heard noises outside. And, in my mind, I created elaborate details to explain those noises, imagining sinister people plotting our demise while we sat helplessly inside. I remember slipping out of bed and pressing my ear to the window to listen. Evil men lurked in the darkness of night, and were seeking the best entry point of our house—or so I was convinced. I'm not sure why I imagined the evil version of Seal Team 6 wanting to invade our home, but I believed it was true. Spoiler alert for those wondering: there were no people plotting. My family and I survived.

While many can chalk my story up to the wild imagination of a young boy, as I've grown older, my propensity to create these stories in my mind has not gone away; it's just different content now. Instead of bad guys invading my home, now I'll tell myself a story about why Ben sent me a text about grabbing coffee. "What's his real motive for meeting?" Or when Lisa asks me a question about something I taught, I may tell myself, "She disagrees with me and her question is setting me up for some gotcha point she wants to make." I'm able to fill the gaps of information in with a story—that may not be accurate at all—but can affect my emotions.

Creating a fictional story in my mind induced that first panic attack. It was a few months after Kaleb's kidneys were removed by accident. I was driving down the interstate and approaching a curve that was sharp for 70 MPH. And out of nowhere, my mind created a scenario of my steering wheel not turning. I careened off the road and crashed. I laid in a coma, but could hear everybody talking. Yet, I had no ability to communicate. As this scenario played out in my mind, I was a half-mile past the curve that triggered the episode. But my heart rate skyrocketed. Sweat saturated my shirt, and my breathing intensified. I later discovered this was the first of many panic attacks I would experience over the next seven years. But how did this happen? I let my mind construct a story that had actual effects on me physically and emotionally.

LOCK'EM UP

Friends, this lesson is key for learning to trust God. We must understand the power of the stories we tell ourselves. Our internal dialogue is consequential. Scripture directs us in monitoring and directing it.

We destroy arguments and every lofty opinion raised against the knowledge of God, and take every thought captive to obey Christ. — 2 Corinthians 10:5

Paul says he destroys arguments and every lofty opinion raised against the knowledge of God. This would include the lies and false stories we tell ourselves. Many preach the lie to themselves that they're left to fate or chance. That's an opinion raised against the knowledge of God and needs to be destroyed. It needs to be put to death.

But notice what Paul says, "Take every thought

captive to obey Christ." To capture something is to imprison it. It's stopping it and preventing it from escaping. Scripture instructs us to take our thoughts captive to obey Christ. We examine our thoughts to ensure they are obedient to Christ's Word. We must scrutinize the stories we tell ourselves and ensure they align with Scripture.

Why should we take thoughts captive? Because if we don't, one thought can give birth to a series of thoughts that spiral our hearts toward the worst-case scenarios. Our thoughts can run wild before we even realize what we're doing. Our thoughts act like a chain of dominoes that begins tipping over. If the first thought isn't obedient to Christ, the thoughts that follow won't be either. And we can create awfully negative stories. We're black-belts at crafting negative stories. We are Stephen King-level at imagining horror stories for our lives.

ROOT AND FRUIT

Those negative stories and thoughts send us into a tailspin of fear, worry, and despair. This is where anxiousness and depression find their source of energy. Fear, anxiousness, worry, and all their related cousins are the fruit that comes from the root of the stories we tell ourselves.

Our lives are like a tree. And the roots of the tree are the thoughts and stories we tell ourselves. If they are in the soil of negative, terrible stories we like to tell ourselves, then the emotional fruit of anxiety, fear, and worry grow. Despair, depression, and panic attacks are fruits, and each has a root. We can almost always trace them back to the stories we tell ourselves.

So what do we do? We take thoughts captive when we see they do not obey the truth of God's Word. We take them captive in obedience to Christ. Even when we've let them get down the road, we must stop them. When we find our thoughts racing, and we're creating scenarios of a future that hasn't happened yet, we stop them. We imprison them.

But then what? The answer isn't to stop thinking thoughts. We can't just say, "I won't think those thoughts anymore." We must replace the thoughts. The Scriptures call this putting off and putting on (Colossians 3). We "put off" our habit to fabricate stories of the future, and we "put on" a different story instead.

The great English pastor, Martyn Lloyd-Jones (1899-1981) once commented on this concept and said, "Have you realized that most of your unhappiness in life is due to the fact that you are listening to yourself instead of talking to yourself?" Instead of listening to the stories we tell ourselves, we need to start purposefully talking to ourselves. Preaching to our hearts.

Our thoughts (roots) must rehearse the truth of God's sovereignty, wisdom, love, and faithfulness. We must preach to ourselves the reality of these things.

When our minds are prone to wander down the road of negative stories, we stop them, and replace them with the truth of Scripture.

Chance doesn't govern our lives. We belong to the Lord, and He sovereignly guides our lives according to His wise plan and love for us. He is faithful to give us all we need along the way, to endure whatever circumstances we face. We preach these truths to ourselves, and the fruit that develops is trust, peace, and contentment.

This happens daily. We can have stray, destructive thoughts come at any moment, regardless of our level of spiritual maturity. Something can happen—a scenario can unfold—and we may fill in the gaps of information with a story that causes us to worry. We must change the story. But don't miss this: Changing the story won't change our circumstances; it changes our perspective.

Imagine your company is laying people off in the coming months. You play out scenarios in your mind of losing your job. You imagine the financial struggle that follows your job loss, and the inability to pay your mortgage. Now you're in your parents' living room embarrassed and asking to borrow money. Before you recognize it, this has all played out in your mind within seconds, and now you're anxious. Fear consumes you.

The moment to capture the thought was the second you imagined losing the job. God holds your future because He's sovereign, and if in His wisdom and love,

He determined to include you in the layoffs, then you trust His plans. Something that hasn't happened shouldn't get permission to control your emotions. Does that mean you do nothing when you hear layoffs discussed? No, you can update your resume, and even consider other jobs to pursue. Trust in the LORD doesn't mean being passive or lazy. It means not letting your mind tell you stories of despair that consume your nerves. None of those things have even happened. But you need to reach a place where those things happening doesn't scare you, because you trust God.

SETTLE IT

How do we get to that place? We preach the truth to ourselves. And we learn how to discern those destructive stories and take them captive. But there's another layer to add.

We need to prepare ourselves in advance of our troubles and trials that we are going to stay the course. We have to remember that trials will come, and when they do, our hearts are prepared to endure the struggles. Just like a boxer prepares for a fight. He knows he's going to get punched. He knows there's going to be pain and swelling. Discomfort will be a part of the process. So they prepare in advance for the pain the match will bring. Christians need to ready ourselves for afflictions. Jesus tells us as much.

Then he said to them, "Nation will rise against nation, and kingdom against kingdom. There will be great earthquakes, and in various places famines and pestilences. And there will be terrors and great signs from heaven. But before all this they will lay their hands on you and persecute you, delivering you up to the synagogues and prisons, and you will be brought before kings and governors for my name's sake. This will be your opportunity to bear witness. Settle it therefore in your minds not to meditate beforehand how to answer, for I will give you a mouth and wisdom, which none of your adversaries will be able to withstand or contradict. —
Luke 21:10-15

There's one major concept I want you to capture from this passage. After warning his disciples that troubles and persecution are coming, Jesus says, "Settle it therefore in your minds not to meditate beforehand how to answer, for I will give you a mouth and wisdom, which none of your adversaries will be able to withstand or contradict." Catch this again: Settle it in your minds.

Jesus tells them trouble is coming, but tells them He will provide what they need when it comes. So His instructions are to settle it in their minds now, not to worry themselves with preparing their responses to threats and authorities. He tells them to: Settle it in your minds now to trust God to sustain you when troubles come. Settle it now, before it comes. So when it comes, you can trust him.

We need to prepare ourselves for suffering, and settle it in our minds before it arrives. You are going to lose people you dearly love in this life. You must settle it in your minds now that Christ will support you in your grief when it comes. Your health will give way and your own life will soon pass. Settle it in your mind now that you will rely on Christ to be your help and strength. You will experience unexpected changes in life that you can't control: job loss, drop in income, relationship troubles, cultural pressure to conform to the world's ways, etc. You must settle it in your minds now, that when these things happen, Christ has promised to provide us what we need. He will guide us, keep us, and help us. We can trust Him.

Don't leave future decisions up to a moment's notice. Decide now that you will be faithful before trial or temptations or troubles come. Settle it now in your minds to trust God instead of leaning on your own understanding.

ICU TEMPTATIONS

I worked through these ideas for several years and embedded them into my life. They got into my bones. Anxiety and panic attacks were a thing of the past. But in October 2017, Kaleb had his strokes and laid unconscious for three weeks. I remember one night sitting in the room after everyone had left. Before I laid down for bed, my mind began creating stories about what our future entailed. As I sat, letting my thoughts run wild, my heart rate increased. This feeling was familiar. The panic attacks had stopped happening several years prior, yet I sat on the hospital pull-out bed on the brink of another one. And I recognized what was happening.

I had a visceral reaction, jerking my posture upright and snapping out of the trance-like state I sat in. I prayed out loud the truths of God's Word. "Lord, help me. I'm going down a rabbit hole of negative thoughts about the future, none of which has happened. I know You hold our lives, including Kaleb's, in Your hands. So whatever Your plans, I know You will walk beside us and sustain us through it." My heart rate slowed. The anxiousness faded. And I went to sleep. Nothing about Kaleb's health or future changed in that moment, but my response did. I chose to trust God instead of leaning on my understanding.

Everything I prayed that night is true. And I can tell you now, many years since that evening, and after Kaleb's death, our God does walk beside us and sustain us. It's not easy. But He's been faithful. He's kept His promises. And we cling tightly to the promises He gives us about our ultimate future in Christ.

I settled in my mind to trust God with our future years before the spiritual battle in the ICU, but I still had to fight to maintain it that evening. And I still fight it daily. To live out Proverbs 3:5-6 is a one-day-at-a-time undertaking. It's not something you check off your list as completed. It's ongoing. It's one day at a time.

Even recently I let my mind drift toward what life would be like forty or fifty years from now. Will my memories with Kaleb still be sharp and crisp? Will they be vague and dim? The thought of being so far removed from those experiences saddened me, and I started dreading it. Then I stopped myself. "No, I will not fret over how good my memories will be in the decades ahead. I'm going to be thankful for today, and trust God for His grace today." And I put the thoughts away. They had nothing to offer me.

DON'T TRUST YOURSELF

Trust God and do not lean on your own understanding. Leaning on your own understanding happens when we try to connect the dots between our circumstances and God's plan. "God's plan for this job loss is to get me to a different job and meet my future spouse." Well, maybe, but nobody can know that. That's one way to lean on your own understanding. Another way is when we tell ourselves negative stories about what our future holds. The stories we create to fill in the gaps of information are prime examples of leaning on our own understanding. Because the stories are our stories. They're our attempts to interpret circumstances. Don't do this! Take these thoughts captive. Stop them in their tracks, and preach to yourself the better story, the true story.

If you are in Christ, you are an adopted child of God, forgiven of sin and loved. He is sovereign over your life. He made you and charted your path, even when and where you'd be born (Acts 17:26). You may have chosen differently if you had the power, but the wisdom of God reminds you that everything flows forth from His knowledge of what is best and His commitment to bring the flourishing of His people. He loves us with a particular love. And that love is never abstract or detached from His personal commitment to be our God, or his will for us to be His people. He keeps His promises to us, and we cling to Him through the uncertainties and pains of life.

When we face the reality of our lack of control, we can either fret and fear, or we can trust the One who is sovereign, wise, and faithful, who loves us and calls us His own. We must recite the right stories and take captive the ones that steal our peace and trust in the LORD. When we trust in the LORD, and not on our own understanding, He promises to make straight our paths. What that means, and how it affects our lives today, is the subject of our next and last chapter.

Discussion Questions

1. Do you tell stories to yourself about how something will go? What are some examples?

2. When you're faced with an uncertain situation, do you find yourself getting anxious or do you rest in the promises of God?

3. Read the following verses and discuss what they tell us about our minds:

> A troubled mind (2 Kings 6:11)
> A depraved mind (1 Timothy 6:5)
> A sinful mind (Romans8:7)
> A dull mind (2 Corinthians 3:14)
> A blinded mind (2 Corinthians 4:4)
> A corrupt mind (2 Timothy 3:8)

4. Why does Paul tell us to take our thoughts captive (2 Corinthians 10:5)? How do we do it? What are we evaluating when we capture thoughts?

5. What does it mean to "put off" and "put on" thoughts? How does the analogy of the tree with its roots and fruits help to understand this practice?

6. How do we "settle in our mind" (Luke 21:14) before we go through trials that we are going to trust the LORD and not lean on our own understanding?

8

WHERE ARE WE HEADED?

We are at the end of our journey. We've sought understanding on how to trust in the Lord with all our hearts. In a world where hurt, pain, and affliction abounds, it isn't easy. But as we've discussed throughout the book, trusting God comes from knowing Him, not pleasant or easy circumstances.

In our primary passage of focus, there are three particular exhortations that we receive. Trust in the LORD with all our your heart. Lean not on your own understanding. In all your ways acknowledge him. Those are the conditions that precede a great promise attached to our passage.

> *Trust in the LORD with all your heart, and do not lean on your own understanding. In all your ways acknowledge him, and he will make straight your paths.*
> *— Proverbs 3:5-6*

Do you see the promise? He will make straight your paths. This is a promise every Christian needs to hear and cling to: He, the Living God, will make your path straight.

The imagery used in the proverb is a "straight path." A path is a track laid down for traveling. Paths lead somewhere. Paths are guides that take us toward a destination. And a straight path implies a clear direction toward a specific destination.

In Nashville, we have three major interstates that come through our city: I-40, I-65, and I-24. If you are driving on an interstate for a long distance, you'll notice curves and changes in direction along the way. However, when you observe the entirety of an interstate from beginning to end, you notice they are straight. They run in straight paths and lead you in clear directions to specific destinations.

But someone must create a path. When we see a road, we assume people constructed it. Someone determined to make it. If we're wandering in the woods and see a path cutting through it, we wouldn't conclude the path was a bizarre manifestation of baldness in the forestry growth. We would conclude someone created the path.

OUR PATH

How does this relate to our focus? Our lives are a walk down a path. Scripture talks about walking with God (Ephesians 4:1; 5:15). Our lives are moving in a direction. Day by day, choice by choice, we're heading in a direction and toward a destination. Everyone is on a path, but not everyone is walking a straight path. Not everyone is traveling a path that leads to life. Some are on a path of destruction.

Proverbs 3:5-6 promises us that God forges and creates the path upon which those who trust Him will travel. It will be straight, meaning it was made with purpose and intentionality. One way to interpret this passage is: quit worrying yourself with trying to play God, and trust that the One who actually is God has your life. Or an even shorter version is, God says, "I got you."

This challenges us to the core of our beliefs and worldview. When we hear "and he will make straight your paths," this question arises: straight paths according to whom? By what standard are we judging this path to be straight? Is it a straight path according to us? Because God has not promised that trusting Him gives you the straight path your flesh wants. Is it a straight path according to the world? Because God hasn't promised to give us what the world calls a straight path. No, when God promises to make our paths straight, it is straight according to Him. It is a straight path according to His will, His desires, His promises, and His plan.

Is that enough for you? Is it enough for you to hear God say, "I'll get you where I want you; I'll accomplish my purposes through your life; and I'll bring you to your Heavenly home?" This strikes at the heart of whether we have truly laid down our lives to worship the Lord. It confronts the core of our beliefs. Do we believe God is the center of the universe, or do we believe we are? Do we suppose God exists for man's glory, or do we exist for God's glory? Do we see suffering as a disruption to our personal happiness to be avoided and escaped at all cost, or do we believe that in God's sovereign wisdom He has purpose even for our pain?

How we answer these questions shapes what we expect a straight path to be and how we interpret what God is promising in these verses.

BUMPY BUT STRAIGHT

Our path is straight. The Lord our God has saved and rescued us from the dominion and power of sin. God rescued us from Satan, Hell, and ourselves. We also have glorious promises of His constant nearness and help, and the reminder that we'll stand in glory for eternity with him.

But let's be honest, we want "straight paths" to mean glassy seas and smooth sailing. We want our straight path to be free of pain, suffering, and sorrows. Most of the daily fears and struggles with worry that consume our thoughts and emotions connect to future unknowns, hurts, and trials. The path ahead presents fears and uncertainties. We know God promises He will make straight our paths, but what if we don't like what God calls straight? We must repent of this me-centered, unbiblical view of life and walking with God.

You will have troubles. Pains and suffering will come. God has purpose for it all. Remember, the world needs redemption. We want everything to unfold smooth and easy, and it's okay to want that. The problem is when we live expecting it. The problem is when we live demanding it. And if we don't get it, we wag the finger at God. This is not biblical Christianity. Biblical Christianity lives sold out to Christ, amazed He reconciled us to God through His finished work, and expectant of our future hope.

We're living between what Christ has already accomplished, and what is still yet to come. Jesus was crucified and raised. He has redeemed and saved us. And we await our future redemption, even as we struggle and suffer while we wait.

PAUL SHOWS THE WAY

The Apostle Paul understood this. He was a denier of Christ and a persecutor of His people. Then Paul came to faith. He couldn't get over God saving him. He understood himself to be a great sinner, and Jesus as a great Redeemer. But why would Jesus save a great sinner like Paul, who caused problems for Christians and actively strove against them whenever he could? He answers that for us.

The saying is trustworthy and deserving of full acceptance, that Christ Jesus came into the world to save sinners, of whom I am the foremost. But I received mercy for this reason, that in me, as the foremost, Jesus Christ might display his perfect patience as an example to those who were to believe in him for eternal life. To the King of the ages, immortal, invisible, the only God, be honor and glory forever and ever. Amen. — 1 Timothy 1:15-18

Paul calls himself the chief of sinners. But Paul also says that he received mercy so that Christ might display his life as an example for others to know they too can believe and have eternal life as well. Seeing Jesus wipe away all of his sin—including his persecution of the church and complicity in Stephen's death (Acts 7)—Paul responds in worship at such grace. Notice, he doesn't feel like he's owed or deserving of anything. It's all God's mercy and kindness, completely undeserved by Paul (or us).

Paul's ministry would take him around the world, traveling from place to place to share the gospel and start churches. As he did so, he experienced hardships and suffering. Think about Paul's ministry. Consider his faithfulness for a moment. He committed his life to taking the gospel to the nations and peoples of the world. But as he did it, he suffered extreme hardship. These were not light trials. He wore the afflictions in his body with scars, and injured limbs. Yet he continued to go. He expounds on his list of sufferings in this snapshot:

Are they servants of Christ? I am a better one—I am talking like a madman—with far greater labors, far more imprisonments, with countless beatings, and often near death. Five times I received at the hands of the Jews the forty lashes less one. Three times I was beaten with rods. Once I was stoned. Three times I was shipwrecked; a night and a day I was adrift at sea; on frequent journeys, in danger from rivers, danger from robbers, danger from my own people, danger from Gentiles, danger in the city, danger in the wilderness, danger at sea, danger from false brothers; in toil and hardship, through many a sleepless night, in hunger and thirst, often without food, in cold and exposure. And, apart from other things, there is the daily pressure on me of my anxiety for all the churches.
— 2 Corinthians 11:23-28

Paul received beatings for the sake of Christ. He suffered hunger, cold, homelessness, and many other afflictions. Instead of seeing these as stains against God, he viewed them as part and parcel on this side of eternity. He saw them as unavoidable realities in a fallen world that is in need of the gospel, Christ's return, and final restoration. Paul's God-oriented perspective shaped his approach to life.

Imagine how distraught we would be if we

experienced anything close to these kinds of afflictions. We would feel sorry for ourselves. We would assume God hated us. We would likely quit, rationalizing that God must not be in it. But Paul saw his life different.

For to me to live is Christ, and to die is gain. If I am to live in the flesh, that means fruitful labor for me. Yet which I shall choose I cannot tell. I am hard pressed between the two. My desire is to depart and be with Christ, for that is far better. — Philippians 1:21-23

His view of life: He belongs to Christ. His life is not his own. If he lives, then he lives to serve Christ in whatever situation he is in. If he dies, it's gain! He desires to be with Christ. Why? Because it is far better! The problem for us is we struggle with believing it is far better. We'll give that answer in Sunday School, but we don't hold it in our hearts. Most Christians desire a comfortable life in a marred creation more than they want to be with Christ. Not Paul. He said, "Give me Christ!" But if he had to remain, then he would serve Christ, because he did not belong to himself. Jesus bought him. He was a *doulos*, a slave, of Christ.

This made him content in all situations. Because he belongs to Christ, and not himself, then he trusts that whatever situation he is in, God placed him there. So he remains content in his trials.

Not that I am speaking of being in need, for I have learned in whatever situation I am to be content. I know how to be brought low, and I know how to abound. In any and every circumstance, I have learned the secret of facing plenty and hunger, abundance and need. I can do all things through him who strengthens me. —
Philippians 4:11-13

Paul is content, whatever the circumstances might be. He doesn't fear tomorrow. He doesn't fret over money, health, or anything else. Why? He has learned contentment in all situations. He discovered the secret: He can do all things through Christ who gives him strength. This isn't a verse about playing basketball beyond your talent level or some other motivational help. This is the secret to surviving through suffering, trials, and afflictions. We can do all things through Christ who strengthens us. As we acknowledge Him, cling to Him, and abide in Him, we can endure the pain and sorrows, because we're supplied with the grace to do so.

Paul knew being with Christ surpassed life on earth. He knew a glorious future awaited that dwarfed all earthly suffering (Romans 8:18; 2 Corinthians 4:17). Heaven awaits the people of God. Jesus overthrows death. Sin will be no more. Resurrection is coming. God will dwell with us forever. That's where our straight path leads.

REST IN HIM

This is the promise of Proverbs 3:5-6. If we trust the LORD, our life now, and forever, is incredibly hopeful. At the heart of it all is full surrender to Christ. This demands more than a Sunday-to-Sunday faith. We must live seeking the Lord above all and treasuring Him above all. If we are in Christ, we belong to Him; our lives are not our own. But He gives us a life-sustaining promise: If we trust the LORD with all of our heart, and lean not on our own understanding, and in all our ways acknowledge Him, He will make straight our paths.

Dear reader, trust in the LORD with your whole heart. The One who is sovereign, wise, and faithful holds it. The One who loves you directs your path. Find your rest in this weary world, in Him.

Discussion Questions

1. Discuss how trusting in the LORD, not leaning on your own understanding and acknowledging God in all your ways will make your path straight.

2. Do you trust the LORD to make your path straight or do you try to straighten it on your own when it seems curvy or bumpy?

3. Is the straight path that God is leading you on enough for you if it doesn't align with the world? What if it costs you a job? Or your savings? Or your health? Or your friends? Or your family?

4. Read 2 Corinthians 11:23-28. Do you think there was something special about Paul that allowed him to endure all of this? What was the real reason Paul could endure (Proverbs 3:5-6)? Do you believe you are endowed with the same Spirit as Paul that would sustain you through the same trials and sufferings?

5. Why is it so important to recognize that the straight path God promises is straight, not according to our definition of straight, but His own?

6. What are some reminders from this chapter about the straight path God has promised His children?

ACKNOWLEDGMENTS

No man labors on an island. Behind every productive and fruitful work comes the help and hands of many people. Some people offer help in different ways, but many people play a part in the process and creation of something. That is true of this book.

A special thanks is owed to Terri McAngus, who read this manuscript multiple times in the editing process. She has eyes like a hawk, and a heart that loves Jesus. Your benefit from this book is tied to her labors.

Another debt of gratitude is due to Josh Wester, who served as the content editor for this project. Josh ensured the ideas were clear, and the message stayed on target for the audience.

Thank you TJC for your support and encouragement to pursue Knowing Jesus Ministries. You are a joy to pastor. And to the elders and staff of TJC, thank you for letting me pursue projects such as these so that more than just members of TJC can benefit from the glories found in the truth of Scripture.

ABOUT THE AUTHOR

Erik is the Founder and Lead Pastor of The Journey Church (tjclive.com) in Lebanon, TN, a church that exists to show Jesus as incomparably glorious. The Journey Church is committed to making gospel rich theology accessible to everyday people. The church reaches a diverse range of people, and continues to grow in both numbers and ministry opportunities to make disciples of Jesus.

He also founded Knowing Jesus Ministries (kjmin.org), a non-profit organization which exists to proclaim timeless truth for everyday life. This ministry provides resources for Christians to grow in their daily walk with Jesus, withstand the onslaught of cultural pressures to conform, and prepare Christians for the suffering that comes in this life. Resources includes books, daily devotions, articles, theology videos, conferences, and weekend respites for families who have lost children.

He's been married to Katrina since 2002, and has three children: Kaleb (who went to be with the Lord on December 1st, 2019), Kaleigh Grace, and Kyra Piper.

Made in the USA
Middletown, DE
15 October 2021